SOMERSET
COUNTRY RECIPES

COMPILED BY
ANN GOMAR

Ravette London

Published by Ravette Limited
3 Glenside Estate, Star Road
Partridge Green, Horsham,
Sussex RH13 8RA
(0403) 710392

Production: Oval Projects Ltd.
Cover design: Jim Wire
Typesetting: Repro-type
Printing & binding: Cox & Wyman Ltd.

Acknowledgements:

Grateful thanks are extended to the many people of Somerset who have contributed towards this collection of recipes, including:

Jim Skeggs for West Buckland Trout

Mrs. S. Pym of Yeovil for Crunchy Currant Accompaniment for Roast Lamb

Mrs Dominey of Vercreech, nr. Castle Cary for Somerset Apple Cake

George & Pilgrims Hotel, Glastonbury for Somerset Bacon Bake, George & Pilgrims Trifle

The Swan Hotel, Wells for Mendip Farm Fry

The Somerset Record Office, Taunton, for Apple Marmalade, Herring Pie, and a number of old handwritten recipes; published with the kind permission of Derek M.M. Shorrocks, County Archivist.

Mary Sirant, Assistant County Historian, County Hall, Taunton, for the Traditional Somerset Quote.

The recipes contained in this book are traditional and many have been compiled from archival sources. Every effort has been made to ensure that the recipes are correct.

RECIPES

SOUPS and BEGINNINGS

Watercress Soup 9
Celery Soup 10
West Country Paté or Potted Meat 11
Mendip Snails 12

FISH

Stuffed Somerset Herrings 13
Trout in Cider (or wine) with Green Sauce 14
Cider Fish Pie with Cheese Topping 15
Herring Pie 16
Salmon Steaks from Exmoor 16
West Buckland Trout 17
Elvers Cake 18
Turbot Steaks with Walnut Sauce 19

POULTRY and GAME

Pigeon Pie 20
Savoury Figgy Pastry 21
Braised Exmoor Venison with Cider and Cream 22
Initialled Venison Pasties from Exmoor 24
Roast Grouse from Exmoor 26
Somerset Casseroled Country Chicken in Cider 27

MEAT

Somerset Shepherd's Pie 28
Rosemary Roast Lamb 29
Crunchy Currant Accompaniment for Roast Lamb 30
Somerset Crocky 30
Cider Liver Casserole 32

Somerset Beef and Beer Stew 33
Mendip Farm Fry 34
Somerset Bacon Bake 35
Priddy Oggies 36
Leek and Bacon or Likky Pie 38
Bacon and Vegetable Stew 39
To Cure Hams 40
Baked Honey Glazed Ham 41
Cider Creamed Pork with Carrots and Mushrooms 42
Bath Chaps 43
Faggots 44

CHEESE DISHES
Somerset Rarebit 45
Cheddar Cheese Omelet 46
Cheddar Cheese Dumplings or Doughboys 47
Creamy Onion Pie with Cheese Pastry 48
Cheddar Cheese Straws 50
Somerset Cheese Bake 51

PUDDINGS
Strawberry Cheesecake 52
Gooseberry Fool 53
Apple Dumplings 54
Castle Pudding from Taunton 55
George & Pilgrims Trifle 56
Somerset Pudding 57
Bilberry (or Whortleberry) and Apple Pie 58
Cider, Raisin or Walnut Pie 59
West Country Junket 60
Somerset Syllabub 61
Bath Ground Rice Pudding or Custard Tart 62
Rice Blancmange 63

CAKES, BUNS and BISCUITS
Honey Iced Somerset Cider Cake 64
Somerset Apple Cake 65
Iced Somerset Apple Sauce Cake 66
Somerset Potato Cake 67
Walnut and Honey Scones 68
Strawberry Shortcake 69
Bath Buns 70
Sally Lunn Buns 72
Walnut and Honey Tarts 73
Sedgemoor Easter Little Cakes 74

SWEETS
Chocolate and Walnut Fudge 75

PRESERVES
Pickled Walnuts 76
Gooseberry Jelly 77
Apple Marmalade 78

SAUCES
Cider Sauce 78

DRINKS
Mulled Cider and Red Wine Punch 79

OLD REMEDY
To Cure ye Bite of a Mad Dog 80

'I've come up from Somerset
Where the cider apple grows'!

Traditional

SOMERSET

Southern Somerset is a county of gently rolling hills and valleys, fertile soil and a favourable climate. Cows graze on the lush pastureland and produce so much rich milk that cream, butter and cheese have always been at the centre of Somerset cooking. Somerset clotted cream is as rich as the neighbouring Cornish and Devon varieties, but has less of a crust.

Cheddar, the small town to the south of the Mendip Hills, near the spectacular Cheddar Gorge, has given its name to a cheese that has become world famous. Cheddar cheese has been made in the same way for hundreds of years. Big cheeses are a Cheddar speciality. In the reign of Queen Elizabeth I, Cheddar cheese was described as the 'best and biggest' in England. The tradition was going strong in 1840, when the biggest recorded Cheddar cheese was made for Queen Victoria's wedding. It was 9ft. wide, weighed 11 cwt. and used the milk from 737 cows. It was made by the farmers of East and West Pennard, villages near Glastonbury. Somerset is also known for other cheese. Ilchester produces a soft cheese with beer and herbs; while Castle Carey makes its own brand.

In the valleys, vegetables, herbs and fruit flourish on the fertile soil — celery, watercress, leeks, onions, carrots, gooseberries, strawberries, walnuts and the most important crop of all, apples.

Dessert, cooker and cider apples are all grown. Traditional varieties of cider apples have wonderful names like Slap ma Girdle, Fox Whelp, Bloody Butcher, Cheatboy and Brown's Apple. On the farms cider apples were allowed to drop from the trees, where they were gathered up and then built into square piles, known as 'cheeses', mixed with straw. The fruit was then pressed by hand, and the juice allowed to ferment naturally.

The local name for cider is scrumpy. As well as being a popular drink, cider is used in Somerset cooking in casseroles, marinades, stocks and for poaching, or to baste a joint to bring out the flavour.

The custom of Wassailling the Apple Trees, which dates back to pagan times, still takes place in Somerset. Legend believes that it guarantees a good crop. A Wassail Queen pours cider round the roots of the trees to encourage growth, while a Wassail song is sung. Then cider soaked toast is put in the branches for the birds, who represent the good spirits. Finally guns are fired to drive away evil spirits from the crop.

Honey was first produced in the West Country in monastries set up by Irish monks who settled in the region.

Somerset is steeped in legend and mystery. It is said that King Arthur of Camelot was carried to die on Glastonbury Tor — the fairy Isle of Avalon. It is fitting therefore the learn that 'Avalon' comes from the Celtic word for 'An Island of Apples'.

In the heart of Somerset are the levels — low heathlands — which have been reclaimed from the sea. Today Somerset has forty miles of coastline. The fens are criss-crossed with dykes, known locally as rhines. The rich peaty soil provides good grazing for many sheep. As well as giving delicious meat, the sheep are used in the local sheepskin industry. Exmoor, which became a royal forest a thousand years ago, today is a National Park part in Somerset, part in Devon. Red deer, grouse and sheep roam freely on the heathland, and in the famous Doone Valley. Jacob's sheep are a black and white breed local to Yeovil, a town in the south, whose ancient name was St. Ivel.

The dramatic limestone Mendip Hills have given their name to a variety of edible snails, which are thought to have been first introduced to Somerset by the Romans. The spa of Bath has been renowned for the therapeutic and mineral properties of its waters since Roman times, when it was called Aquae Sulis. This beautiful city is still a famous spa, but also has a reputation for good food. It has produced more local specialities than any other city in England, except perhaps the capital, London. Bath is famous for Bath Buns, Bath Wigs (a narrow bread roll made with milk), Bath Chaps, Bath Olivers, Bath Polony (a sausage with a delicate flavour and a bright red skin), and Sally Lunn Buns.

WATERCRESS SOUP

Serves 4

This soup is also delicious in the summer served chilled, and garnished with sprigs of watercress instead of cheese.

½ lb (225 g) chopped watercress
½ lb (225 g) potatoes
2 small onions
1 oz (25 g) butter or margarine
1½ pts (900 ml/ 3¾ cups) milk
1 pt (600 ml/ 2½ cups) water
Salt and pepper
1 oz (25 g) Cheddar cheese
½ teaspoon nutmeg
¼ pt (150 ml/ ⅔ cup) double cream

Remove any thick stalks and discoloured leaves from the watercress. Wash thoroughly and leave to drain.

Peel the potatoes and cut into thick slices. Peel and slice the onions.

Put the potatoes and onions in the water, bring to the boil and simmer for 15 minutes or until very soft.

Rub the potatoes and onions through a sieve. Strain, keeping the cooking liquid in a bowl.

Melt the fat in a saucepan.

Add the watercress and cook gently for 3 minutes without browning.

Stir in the potato and onion mixture.

Gradually add the water in which the vegetables were boiled and the milk. Simmer for 15 mintues.

Rub through a sieve again or blend in a blender.

Reheat the soup, stir in the nutmeg, and season to taste.

Blend in the cream and sprinkle the cheese on top of the soup before serving very hot.

CELERY SOUP WITH SIPPETS

Serves 6

In former centuries the main meal for many country men and women was a pottage of vegetables, often favoured imaginatively with herbs, with perhaps a little meat if they were lucky. The pottage or broth was eaten with hunks of bread.

3 heads of celery
1 large potato
1 onion
1 pint (600 ml/ 2½ cups) white stock
1 pint (600 ml/ 2½ cups) milk
1 oz (25 g) margarine
1 oz (25 g) flour
Salt and pepper
2 fl oz (3 tablespoons/ ¼ cup) cream

Remove the outer stalks and green parts of the celery. Wash the remainder and chop into 1 inch pieces.

Peel and chop the onion. Peel and slice the potato.

Melt the margarine in a saucepan. Put in the chopped celery, onion and potato and fry gently for a few mintues. Do not let them acquire any colour.

Stir in the flour and cook for a further two minutes, stirring. Gradually add the stock, still stirring.

Season with salt and pepper to taste. Bring to the boil and then cover and simmer gently for about 30 minutes or until the celery is quite soft.

Rub the soup through a sieve or blend in a liquidizer.

Return to the saucepan, add the milk and bring back to the boil.

Remove from the heat and swirl in the cream. Serve with sippets.

To make fried sippets:

Cut stale bread into small cubes. Put the bread cubes into a frying basket. Fry in hot oil until golden brown.

WEST COUNTRY PATÉ OR POTTED MEAT

Serves 12

The Old English term for the french word paté, is 'potted' — a smooth or coarse rich paste.

½ lb (225 g) streaky bacon rashers
1 lb (450 g) chicken livers
1 lb (450 g) pork or pork sausagemeat
1 onion
1 teaspoon salt
½ teaspoon ground black pepper
½ teaspoon dried thyme
2 cloves garlic, crushed
2 tablespoons brandy
2 tablespoons double cream

Remove the rinds of bacon. Stretch the rashers on a board with a tableknife.

Line the bottom of a 2 pt ovenproof dish or a 2 lb (1 kg) loaf tin with the rashers.

Cut up the chicken liver, and the pork into small pieces. Chop the onion finely. Mix the ingredients together.

Put the mixture through a mincer, using the finest cutters.

Stir in the salt, pepper, thyme and garlic. Stir in the brandy and cream.

Pack the mixture into the dish or tin, and level the top.

Cover with a foil lid and cook in the oven for 2 hours.

Remove from the oven. Leave in the tin and place weights on top of the paté.

Leave for about 8 hours or overnight in the refrigerator.

Remove the weight and foil. The paté can either be turned out or served from the ovenproof dish it was cooked in.

Oven: 325°F/160°C Gas Mark 3

MENDIP SNAILS

Serves 3

It is said that edible snails were first brought to Somerset by the Romans. Today they are collected in the Mendip Hills and sold in the local markets. The Somerset name for these molluscs is 'wallfish'.

In Somerset the water for cooking snails is often mixed with cider. Cider may be used in the sauce in place of Worcester Sauce.

36 Snails

For the sauce:
4 oz (100 g) butter
1 tablespoon of parsley, chopped
Salt and pepper
1 tablespoon lemon juice
2 shallots
3 tablespoons Worcester sauce

Wash the snails thoroughly by brushing under running water.

Soak them in salt water for 12 hours. Wash again and drain.

Put the snails into a saucepan of boiling water, sufficient to cover them. Simmer for 20 minutes. Strain.

When cool remove the snails from their shells and cut off the black ends.

Dry and keep the shells.

To make the sauce:

Cream the butter. Mix in the chopped parsley and pepper to taste and melt in a saucepan.

Chop the shallots finely and fry them gently, without browning the butter.

Add the brown sauce and the snails.

Season to taste.

Keep the mixture hot.

Put the snails back in the shells covering them with sauce.

STUFFED SOMERSET HERRINGS Serves 4

Traditionally known as the 'poor man's fish', herrings are in fact very nutritious and have a delicate flavour.

4 herrings
2 oz (50 g) double cream
1 small onion
Salt and pepper
½ pt (300 ml/1¼ cups) cider
4 oz (100 g) cottage or Somerset cream cheese

Clean the herrings and cut off the heads, tails and fins.

Split the fish down the back as neatly as possible.

Remove the soft roes, and mash them.

Whip the cream until thick.

Peel and chop the onion finely.

Mix the roes and onion with the cream, and season with salt and pepper to taste.

Put the roe stuffing into the slits down the back of the fish.

Place the fish in a frying pan.

Pour the cider over the fish.

Bring to the boil, and then poach the fish slowly in the cider until cooked, turning gently with a fish slice if recquired.

Remove the fish and place on a serving dish.

Allow the cider liquid to cool.

Beat the cider liquid and the cottage or cream cheese together to form a sauce.

Pour over the fish.

Garnish with cucumber slices.

TROUT IN CIDER (OR WINE) WITH GREEN SAUCE

Serves 6

6 trout
1 pint (600 ml/2½ cups) water
½ pint (300 ml/1¼ cups) dry cider (or white wine)
Small bunch of parsley
Bay leaf
Salt and pepper
2 tablespoons double cream
1 cup of mayonnaise
1 tablespoon chives
Small bunch of watercress (or spinach)
Lemon

Put the clean and gutted fish in a shallow pan.

Pour on the water and cider.

Add the salt and pepper to taste.

Add the parsley and bay leaf.

Bring slowly to simmering point.

Simmer gently for 10-15 minutes until fish is cooked.

Gently lift the fish out and arrange on a serving dish.

Finely chop the chives.

Remove the stalks from the watercress, and finely chop the leaves.

Blend the mayonnaise with the double cream, chopped chives and watercress in a blender, or mix together thoroughly in a bowl.

Serve the trout hot or cold decorated with quarters of freshly cut lemon, and with the green sauce in a separate dish.

CIDER FISH PIE WITH CHEESE TOPPING

Serves 4

1 lb (450 g) fresh haddock or cod
Salt and pepper
5 tomatoes
4 oz (100 g) mushrooms
¾ pint (450 ml/ 2 cups) cider
1 oz (25 g) butter or margarine
1 oz (25 g) flour
3 oz (75 g) Cheddar cheese

Skin and slice four tomatoes. Slice the mushrooms.

Season the fish with salt and pepper and poach gently in a saucepan with the tomatoes and mushrooms in the cider for about 10 minutes or until cooked.

Strain and keep the liquid.

Put the vegetables into a casserole dish.

Flake the fish and remove any skin and bones.

Mix the flaked fish gently with the vegetables.

Melt the fat in a saucepan. Mix in the flour and cook for a few moments stirring.

Gradually add the liquid, still stirring.

Bring to the boil, and then simmer the sauce for a few minutes.

Pour the sauce over the fish and vegetables.

Grate the cheese, and sprinkle on top of the casserole.

Slice the remaining tomato and place on top of the casserole.

Brown the dish in a hot oven until the cheese is brown and bubbling, and the tomato slices cooked.

Garnish with parsley before serving.

Oven: 450°F/230°C Gas Mark 8 to brown.

HERRING PIE

An old handwritten unpublished recipe in the Somerset Record Office at Taunton.

Having scaled gutted and washed your herrings clean cut off their heads fins and tails make a good crust cover your dish and season your herrings with beaten mace pepper and salt and put a little butter in the bottom of your dish and then the herrings. Over these put some apples and onions sliced very thin put some butter on the top then pour a little water lay on the lid send it to the oven and let it be well cooked.

SALMON STEAKS FROM EXMOOR

Fresh salmon is best grilled.

1 salmon steak ¾ inch thick serves one person.

Place the salmon steaks on a grid and place under a hot grill.

Cook on one side for about 5 minutes.

Turn over and grill for a further 4 minutes, or until cooked.

Serve hot with vegetables or cold with salad.

Garnish with lemon wedges and sliced cucumber.

WEST BUCKLAND TROUT

Serves 1

West Buckland is a village near Wellington, in Somerset.

1 small wild trout
Up to ½ lb (255 g) mushrooms
Parsley
Slice of white bread
Butter
Tarragon to taste
Seasoned flour
Slices of lemon

Prepare the fish.

Mix the tarragon with the butter and place in the fish's belly.

Dip the fish in the seasoned flour to coat.

Wrap the fish in greaseproof paper.

Place the parcel under the hot grill, and grill until the paper chars.

Chop the mushrooms finely.

Fry gently in butter.

Fry the bread until golden brown.

Unwrap the trout, and arrange it on the bread with the mushrooms.

Pour the butter fat and juices over the fish before serving very hot.

Garnish with lemon slices and finely chopped parsley.

ELVERS CAKE

Serves 6

Elvers (baby eels) are prized as a great delicacy in Somerset. Schools of elvers on their way up the River Severn are caught on the Spring tides at night by Somerset fishermen. They are also caught in the brines or drainage channels on Sedgemoor.

Eels are believed to spawn in the Sargasso Sea in the Atlantic. The young undertake a long migratory journey, where those that escape capture grow to maturity in estuarys and rivers, particularly in the West Country. After a number of years, now a silvery colour, the mature eels journey back to the Sargasso Sea to begin their life cycle again. In olden days, elvers were sold in street markets. Today most are sent to breeding farms, although some are prepared as traditional specialities.

2 lbs (1 kg) elvers
Salt and pepper
1 lb (450 g) shortcrust pastry
1 egg

Wash the elvers thoroughly and dry them.

Season with salt and pepper.

Roll out the pastry.

Place the elvers in the middle of the pastry.

Wrap over the pastry to make a neat parcel, sealing the edges with water.

Put the pastry parcel on a greased baking sheet.

Beat the egg.

Brush the pastry with the beaten egg.

Bake in a hot oven for 25 minutes.

Cut into individual slices.

Oven: 450°F/230°C Gas Mark 8

TURBOT STEAKS WITH WALNUT SAUCE

Serves 6

6 turbot steaks
1 pt (600 ml/ 2½ cups) water or sufficient to cover the fish
2 oz (50 g) butter
2 oz (50 g) flour
9 pickled walnuts
Salt and pepper
Pickled walnuts and watercress to garnish

Put the fish steaks in a pan and cover with water.

Bring to the boil and poach gently for 20 minutes.

Take the turbot steaks out of the pan and arrange on a serving dish.

Keep warm.

Strain and retain the fish stock.

Melt the butter in a saucepan.

Stir in the flour.

Cook without browning for a few minutes, still stirring.

Gradually stir in ½ pt (300 ml/ 1¼ cups) of the strained fish stock.

Bring the sauce to the boil and simmer for a few minutes, until it thickens, still stirring.

Mash the walnuts and add them to the sauce.

Season with salt and pepper to taste, and cook for a few minutes more.

Pour the sauce over the fish.

Serve garnished with watercress and halved pickled walnuts.

PIGEON PIE

Serves 6

Pigeon pie is a very old English speciality. In earlier times nearly every household had a pigeon cote to supply the family with fresh meat when no other was available.

12 oz (350 g) shin of beef
4 oz (100 g) ox kidney
½ pint (300 ml/1¼ cups) brown stock plus an extra ¼ pint (150 ml/⅔ cup) if pie is to be served cold (or sufficient to cover ingredients in pie)
2 pigeons
2 onions
4 shallots
3 teaspoons chopped parsley
3 eggs
Salt and pepper
8 oz (225 g) puff pastry
½ oz (15 g) gelatine — if pie is to be served cold.

Cut up the beef and kidney into small cubes.

Put the meat into a saucepan with the stock.

Bring to the boil and simmer until tender.

Strain and retain the stock.

Cut the pigeons into joints.

Slice the onions and shallots.

Hard boil 2 of the eggs, shell and slice.

Season with salt and pepper.

Build up alternative layers of steak and kidney, onion, shallot, parsley, hard boiled egg and pigeon in a pie dish.

Pour the stock over the mixture to come about half way up the pie dish.

Roll out the pastry on a floured board.

Cover the pie dish with a pastry lid and flute edges.

Make a slit in the top for the steam to escape.

Beat the remaining egg yolk, and brush the top of the pie.

Bake in a moderate oven.

Oven: 450°F/225°C Gas Mark 7 for 10 minutes
Reduce to: 350°F/175°C Gas Mark 4 for 40 minutes

If the pie is to be served cold mix ¼ pint (150 ml/⅔ cup) with ½ oz (15 g) powdered gelatine.

When the pie is out of the oven but before it is cold, pour the stock through the steam vent.

Allow to become completely cold before serving.

SAVOURY FIGGY PASTRY

Figgy pastry traditionally covered Somerset rook pie which was once a popular speciality, made in May when farmers culled the large populations in the rookeries.

As many as 12 rooks would be needed to make an average pie, as only the breasts were used mixed with pieces of fat bacon. The pie or pudding covered with the figgy pastry was steamed for three hours, and served with gooseberry jelly. Figgy pastry can be used today to cover a rabbit pie or chicken pie.

8oz (225 g) self-raising flour
Salt and pepper
4 oz (100 g) margarine
2 oz (50 g) currants
2 oz (50 g) stoned raisins
Water to mix

Sieve the flour with the salt and pepper to taste.

Stir in the dried fruit.

Add sufficient water to give a stiff dough.

Roll out on a floured board.

BRAISED EXMOOR VENISON WITH CIDER AND CREAM SAUCE

Serves 4

Venison is the meat of the deer. Deer are to be found in Exmoor. As venison is game, make sure it has been well hung before cooking. Venison can be bought in season from butchers dealing in game. Venison meat is sometimes rather dry. Marinating overcomes this.

1½ lb (675 g) venison meat (as it is being braised it does not need to be the best cut)
½ lb (225 g) bacon
2 onions
6 oz (175 g) butter or margarine
2 oz (50 g) flour
1 lemon
Salt and pepper
¼ pt (150 ml/ ⅔ cup) single cream
4 oz (100 g) mushrooms
Watercress

For the marinade:
1 pint (600 ml/ 2½ cups) cider
1 bouquet garni sachet

Add the bouquet garni to the cider.

Lay the meat in the marinade and leave for at least 4 hours or longer.

Remove the meat from the marinade, and cut into suitable portions.

Peel and slice the onions.

Chop the bacon into small pieces.

Melt 4 oz (100 g) of the fat in a frying pan.

Fry the meat in the hot fat to seal it on all sides.

Remove the meat.

Fry the onions and the bacon until soft.

Put the onions and the bacon into a casserole.

Lay the venison on top.

Lightly season the meat with salt and pepper.

Squeeze the lemon, and pour the juice over the meat.

Sprinkle the meat with flour.

Pour in enough of the marinade to almost cover the meat, and mix in the flour.

Put a lid tightly on the casserole.

Cook in a moderate oven for 2 hours.

Remove the casserole from the oven, and take out the meat.

Keep the meat hot on a serving dish.

Put the liquid in a saucepan.

Strain if preferred.

Add a stock cube to the liquid and reduce it by boiling to the required consistency.

Season to taste.

Stir in the cream.

Pour the sauce over the meat.

Serve garnished with mushrooms lightly cooked in 2 oz (50 g) of butter in a saucepan, and watercress.

Oven: 350°F/180°C Gas Mark 4

INITIALLED VENISON PASTIES FROM EXMOOR

Makes 4 large pasties

Pasties originated in Cornwall. For centuries they were the mainstay of the working man's midday meal. It was particulary popular among the wives of Cornish tin miners, as an ideal filling, nutritious, easily carried, complete meal. Pasties were robust enough to survive being put in the miner's pocket.

They are now universally popular, and are still a very good dish for lunch or supper, served with a salad or hot vegetables, and are also ideal for packed meals or picnics. Venison can be bought in season from butchers dealing in game.

1 lb (450 g) shortcrust pastry
1 lb (450 g) lean, raw venison
1 lb (450 g) raw potato
8 oz (255 g) raw onion
Salt and pepper
A little water
1 egg

Roll the pastry out on a floured board to about ¼ inch thick.

Cut into four rounds about 8 inch in diameter.

(An inverted plate acts as a useful template)

Cut the meat into very small pieces.

Peel the potato and dice into very small pieces.

Chop the onion finely.

Mix all the ingredients together.

Season with salt and pepper.

Moisten the mixture very slightly with a little water.

Pile the mixture evenly in the centre of the pastry rounds.

Moisten the edges of the pastry.

Draw the pastry up to meet on top of the filling.

Seal the 'envelope' by crimping the edges together firmly.

To crimp: With fingers, turn over small folds all round the edge — rather like 'dog-earing' a book.

Make a hole with a knife in each pasty to allow steam to escape.

Cut the initials of the diners from the pastry scraps.

Stick to one end of each pastry with a little water.

This was the custom in West Country families — presumably so that if a meal was unfinished, it could be enjoyed later by the rightful owner!

Beat the egg, and use to brush each pasty.

Bake in the oven until golden brown.

Serve hot or cold.

Oven: 425°F/220°C Gas Mark 7 for 10 minutes
Reduce to: 325°F/160°C Gas Mark 3 for 45 minutes

ROAST GROUSE FROM EXMOOR Serves 2

These popular game birds come into season on the 12th August. The season lasts until the end of November. Grouse can be bought at butchers that deal in game.

1 grouse — grouse usually weigh up to 1 lb (450 g)
2 oz (50 g) butter
Salt and pepper
1 slice of bread
Thin rashers of streaky bacon, if required
Fat for roasting
Watercress to garnish

Pluck, draw and truss the bird in the same way as any fowl, or ask your butcher to do it.

Put 1 oz (25 g) of butter inside the bird, and use the rest to butter the outside.

(Thin slices of bacon can be tied over the breast as an extra protection.)

Season with salt and pepper.

Melt the fat in a roasting tin, and seal the bird on all sides.

Place in a hot oven for 5 minutes, then reduce to a moderate heat and roast for 25 minutes, basting frequently.

Toast the bread and remove the crusts.

A few minutes before serving, place the grouse on the toast on a serving dish.

Serve with brown gravy made from game stock in a separate dish.

Garnish with watercress.

Oven: 400°F/200°C Gas Mark 6 for 5 minutes
Reduce to: 350°F/180°C Gas Mark 4 for 25 minutes

SOMERSET CASSEROLED COUNTRY CHICKEN IN CIDER

Serves 4

4 chicken joints
3 oz (75 g) flour
Salt and pepper
2 fl oz (3 tablespoons/ ¼ cup) oil
4 rashers bacon
2 onions
8 oz (225 g) can of tomatoes
½ teaspoon oregano or mixed herbs
¼ pint (150 ml/ ⅔ cup) dry cider
¼ pint (150 ml/ ⅔ cup) chicken stock
Bay leaf
Parsley

Coat the chicken joints in seasoned flour.

Melt the fat in a frying pan.

Fry the chicken until golden brown on all sides.

Chop the onions and cut the bacon into pieces.

Remove the chicken and put in a casserole.

Fry the onions and bacon gently for a few minutes.

Add to the casserole.

Stir the remaining flour into the fat (should be about 1 tablespoon) in frying pan, cook for 1 minute still stirring.

Add the tomatoes, herbs, cider, stock and bay leaf.

Bring to the boil, sirring. Cook until sauce thickens.

Pour over the chicken.

Cover casserole and cook in moderate oven for about 1 hour.

Remove bay leaf before serving sprinkled with chopped parsley.

Oven: 350°F/180°C Gas Mark 4

SOMERSET SHEPHERD'S PIE

Serves 4

1 lb (450 g) lamb or mutton
1 onion
1 tablespoon of oil
1 oz (25 g) flour
¼ pint (150 ml/⅔ cup) meat stock
½ teaspoon mixed herbs
Salt and pepper
1 lb (450 g) potatoes

Cook and mash the potatoes with a little milk and butter.

Heat the oil in a frying pan.

Peel and slice the onion.

Mix with the meat.

Lightly fry the meat and onions.

Stir in the flour, stock, herbs and seasoning.

Pack the mixture into an ovenproof dish.

Spread the mashed potato over the meat and make a pattern on the surface with a fork.

Note: The uneven surface will brown unevenly in the oven, and is a feature of the dish.

Bake in a moderate oven for 45 minutes, or until golden brown.

Decorate with parsley sprigs before serving.

Oven: 350°F/180°C Gas Mark 4

ROSEMARY ROAST LAMB

Serves 4

2 lbs (1 kg) breast of lamb
Salt and pepper
1 sprig or 1 teaspoon dried rosemary
1 bay leaf
1 oz (25 g) butter or margarine
½ pint (300 ml/ 1¼ cups) meat stock
1 dessertspoon cornflour
1 tablespoon water

Season the joint with the salt and pepper.

Put the meat into a baking tin that holds the joint comfortably but is not too large.

Add the rosemary and bay leaf to the stock and pour it into the tin.

Spread the fat onto the top of the joint.

Cover with buttered greaseproof paper.

Bake for ¾ hour.

Remove the paper.

Bake for a further 15 minutes until the meat is nicely brown.

Remove from the oven.

Place the joint on a serving dish.

Strain any fat from the gravy and remove the rosemary sprig and bay leaf.

Mix the cornflour to a cream with the water.

Stir into the gravy, and simmer for a few minutes until it thickens.

Serve the gravy with roast the meat.

Oven: 375°F/190°C Gas Mark 5

CRUNCHY CURRANT ACCOMPANIMENT FOR ROAST LAMB

6 ozs (175 g) self-raising flour
3 oz (75 g) suet or margarine if preferred
A pinch of salt
3 oz (75 g) currants
1 teaspoon baking powder
A little milk to bind

Rub the fat into the flour until the mixture resembles breadcrumbs.

Stir in the salt and the teaspoon of baking powder.

Stir in the currants.

Bind the mixture together with sufficient milk to give a stiff mixture.

Put into a greased dish.

Bake in the oven for 1 hour with roasting joint until brown and crunchy on top.

SOMERSET CROCKY

Serves 6

This dish is traditionally called Pot Pie in other counties.

Beef or veal can be used instead of lamb. If using beef, omit the apples. The potatoes may be omitted if preferred.

1¾ lb (800 g) lamb
2 oz (50 g) flour
2 oz (50 g) oil
3 onions
1 lb cooking apples
Salt and pepper
1 pt (600 ml/ 2½ cups) meat stock
1 lb (450 g) potatoes
8 oz (225 g) puff pastry

Cut the meat into 1 inch cubes.

Roll the meat in the flour.

Heat the oil in a frying pan.

Fry the meat in the hot fat. Remove the meat.

Fry the onions until golden brown. Remove the onions.

Peel, core and slice the apples.

Put the meat, onions and apples in layers in a casserole or pie dish, seasoning the meat layers with salt and pepper.

Pour on the stock to three quarters cover the mixture.

Cover the dish with a lid or foil and cook in a moderate oven for 1½ hours or until the meat is tender.

Peel and thickly slice the potatoes.

Gently parboil them in salted water until just soft. Strain.

When the meat is ready, remove the dish from the oven.

Take off lid and allow meat to cool slightly.

Add more stock if required.

Put the potatoes on top of the meat.

Roll out the puff pastry. Cover the dish with a pastry lid.

Make a hole in the centre of the pastry for the steam to escape.

Increase the oven temperature.

Return dish to oven and cook for 25-30 minutes until the pastry is golden brown.

Serve garnished with parsley.

Oven: 350°F/180°C Gas Mark 4 for 1½ hours
Increase to: 400°F/200°C Gas Mark 6 for 25-30 minutes

CIDER LIVER CASSEROLE

Serves 4

1 lb (450 g) lambs liver
2 oz (50 g) flour
Salt and pepper
4 rashers bacon
2 medium onions
A little oil for frying
4 tomatoes
¼ pint (150 ml/ ⅔ cup) meat stock
¼ pint (150 ml/ ⅔ cup) cider

Slice the liver.

Mix the flour with salt and pepper to taste.

Roll the liver in the seasoned flour and coat thoroughly.

Cut the bacon into small pieces, after removing the rinds.

Peel and slice the onions.

Heat the fat in a frying pan.

Gently fry the liver both sides for a minute or two.

Remove the liver and put in an ovenproof dish.

Lightly fry the bacon and onions.

Remove and add to the liver and tomatoes.

Skin and slice the tomatoes and place on top of the liver.

Mix the stock with the cider.

Stir in a little more flour if required to thicken the cooking juices in the frying pan. Then gradually add the liquid.

Bring to the boil and simmer for a few minutes.

Pour over the liver and cover with a lid or foil.

Bake in a moderate oven for 1 hour.

Oven: 350°F/180°C Gas Mark 4

SOMERSET BEEF AND BEER STEW Serves 5

Beer used in cooking should be of room heat, not chilled, and is best slightly flat.

1½ lb (675 g) stewing steak
2 onions
3 oz (75 g) margarine or butter
3 oz (75 g) plain flour
½ pint (300 ml/ 1¼ cups) draught beer
½ pint (300 ml/ 1¼ cups) beef stock
Salt and pepper

Peel and slice the onions.

Melt the fat in a frying pan.

Fry the onions until soft.

Drain and put into a casserole.

Cut the beef into 1 inch cubes.

Roll the meat in 2 oz (50 g) of seasoned flour.

Fry the meat in the fat until brown on all sides.

Put the meat into the casserole with the onions.

Stir in the remaining 1 oz (25 g) of flour to the fat in the frying pan.

Cook, stirring for a few moments.

Gradually stir in the stock, beer, herbs and seasoning to taste.

Bring to the boil.

Pour over the meat in the casserole.

Cover tightly.

Cook in a slow oven for 2 hours.

Oven: 325°F/160°C Gas Mark 3

MENDIP FARM FRY

A delicious pork recipe from The Swan Hotel at Wells — a 15th century coaching inn facing the magnificent West front of Wells Cathedral, which displays the most extensive array of medieval sculptures in the British Isles. Every day at 4 pm the swans of Wells Cathedral ring the gatehouse bell for food.

1½ lbs (675 g) belly pork
¼ lb (100 g) brown sugar
¾ pt (450 ml/ 2 cups) natural dry cider
3 cloves
Seasoning
Oil for frying

Slice the belly pork.

Fry the belly pork until slightly browned.

Lay in a deep baking dish and cover with the brown sugar.

Boil the cider with the cloves and seasoning until ½ reduced.

Add the cider to the belly pork.

Bake in a hot oven for 15 minutes.

Serve with pan fry potatoes and spring greens.

Oven: 400°F/200°C Gas Mark 6

SOMERSET BACON BAKE

This is a dish served at the ancient George and Pilgrims Hotel, Glastonbury, which has offered hospitality for more than 500 years. Behind the ecclesiastical stone frontage and mullioned windows there are old timber beams adorned by carved angels and guarded by death masks of monks, as well as good food and comfort.

1 onion, sliced
8 oz (225 g) ham, sliced
6 oz (175 g) potato
6 oz (175 g) peas
2 pints (1.15 litres/5 cups) bechamel sauce
4 oz (100 g) mushrooms, sliced
1 hardboiled egg, sliced
Grated Cheddar cheese

Fry the sliced onion until cooked soft.

Add the sliced ham, potato and peas.

Make up two pints of bechamel sauce.

Add to the above ingredients.

Add the sliced mushrooms.

Put in a baking tray 2 inches (5 cm) deep.

Cover with slices of hardboiled egg and grated cheese.

Bake for approximately 20 minutes in a hot oven.

Oven: 375°F/190°C Gas Mark 5

PRIDDY OGGIES

Makes 8 pasties

In Somerset the Cornish Tiddy Oggie or potato pasty has been adapted to include the local cheese and pork. The speciality is named after the Somerset village of Priddy in the Mendip Hills, between Cheddar and Wookey Hole, near Wells.

Priddy Oggies made to an original recipe are served at the Miners Arms in Priddy.

For the cheese pastry:

1 lb (450 g) plain flour
4 oz (100 g) margaine
4 oz (100 g) lard
½ teaspoon salt
½ teaspoon dry mustard
6 oz (175 g) Cheddar cheese, finely grated
2 egg yolks
A little water if required

For the filling:

1 lb (450 g) pork fillet
8 rashers of smoked bacon
8 oz (225 g) Cheddar cheese
½ teaspoon thyme or dried mixed herbs
Salt and black pepper
2 eggs

Sieve the flour and salt together.

Rub the fat into the flour until it resembles fine bread-crumbs.

Add the pepper and dry mustard.

Stir in the grated cheese.

Beat the egg yolks together.

Mix to a stiff dough with the egg yolks, adding water if required.

Rest the pastry in the refrigerator before rolling out on a floured board, and cutting into eight rectangular pieces.

To make the pork and bacon filling:

Beat the pork fillet to a thickness of about ¼ inch.

Cut into eight portions.

Put the pork fillets on the pastry rectangles.

Take the rinds off the bacon and cut it up into eight portions.

Lay the bacon on top of the meat.

Grate the cheese into a bowl.

Stir in the herbs and season with salt and pepper.

Beat the eggs.

Use half the eggs or sufficient to bind the cheese mixture.

Spread the mixture over the meat and bacon.

Dampen the pastry edges with water.

Draw up round the filling.

Seal and flute to give a scalloped effect.

Brush the oggies with the remaining beaten egg.

Bake in a hot oven for 30 minutes until golden brown.

Test whether the meat is cooked with a skewer — if it requires longer cooking and the pastry is done, protect with greaseproof paper.

Oven: 400°F/200°C Gas Mark 6 for 10 minutes
Reduce to: 350°F/180°C Gas Mark 4 for 30 minutes

LEEK AND BACON OR LIKKY PIE

This dish is called in Somerset and thoughout the West County — Likky or Leeky Pie.

1 lb (450 g) leeks
8 oz (225 g) streaky or bacon pieces
Salt and pepper
¼ pint (150 ml/⅔ cup) milk
2 eggs
8 oz (225 g) puff pastry
2 fl oz (3 tablespoons/¼ cup) single cream

Wash the leeks throughly and chop into rings.

Cut the bacon into small pieces.

Mix the leeks and bacon together.

Season to taste.

Put the leeks and bacon in a saucepan.

Cover with milk and bring to the boil.

Simmer gently for 20 minutes.

Allow to cool.

Separate the eggs. Beat the yolks together with the cream.

Whisk the whites until stiff and fold into the yolks.

Add to the leeks and bacon.

Put the mixture into a pie dish.

Roll out the pastry on a floured board.

Cover the pie dish with pastry, fluting the edges.

Make a small slit in the centre of the pie to allow the steam to escape.

Bake in a hot oven for 30 minutes or until golden brown.

Oven: 400°F/200°C Gas Mark 6

BACON AND VEGETABLE STEW Serves 6

2 lbs (1 kg) bacon forelock joint
1 lb (450 g) potatoes
4 onions
6 carrots
1 turnip
1 lb (450 g) apples
Pepper
Dry mustard
½ pint (300 ml/ 1¼ cups) dry cider
½ pint (300 ml/ 1¼ cups) water
2 oz (50 g) Cheddar cheese

Cut the bacon up into 1 inch cubes.

Peel and slice the potatoes, carrots, turnip and apples.

Starting with a layer of bacon, and finishing with a layer of overlapping potatoes, put the meat, vegetables and apples into a fireproof dish or saucepan.

Sprinkle each layer (except the apples) with a little salt and mustard.

Mix the cider and water together.

Pour over the meat, vegetables and apples to come just level with the top layer of potatoes. If necessary, add extra cider and water.

Bring to the boil.

Simmer gently with the lid on for 1 hour or until cooked.

If dish has been cooked in a saucepan, put into a casserole for serving.

Grate the cheese and sprinkle over the potato topping.

Brown in a hot oven until the cheese is brown and bubbling before serving.

Oven: 375°F/190°C Gas Mark 5
450°F/230°C Gas Mark 8 to brown

To Cure Hams

A handwritten recipe from the Somerset Record Office, Taunton.

A ham from 18-20 lbs is to be salted with common salt and lay 2 or 3 days to let the bloody brine run from it then take 1½ lbs of treackle 1 lb of Bay salt ½ lb of common salt 2 oz of Salt Petre 1 oz of black pepper put these together in a saucepan and mix them well and when it is very hot take and rub it well with your hands into the ham it lay in the pickle a month turning it and basting it every day then take it out of the pickle and hang it up to smoke in a chimney where there is a wood fire for 3 weeks afterwards put in a paper bag in a dry place it may be dressed in three months but it is better if kept for 4 months or one year.

BAKED HONEY GLAZED HAM

4 lbs (1.75 kg) piece of gammon

For the glaze:
4 oz (100 g) honey
4 oz (100 g) brown sugar
5 fl oz (150 ml/⅔ cup) orange juice

Soak the gammon in cold water overnight.

Wipe the joint dry.

Weigh and wrap in foil.

Put the gammon in a baking tin.

Bake in a moderate oven for approximately 1 hour 40 minutes (allow 20 minutes per lb, and 20 minutes extra according to the weight after soaking).

15 minutes before the end of the cooking time, take the ham out of the oven.

Remove the foil.

Strip off all the outer rind.

Score the white surface of fat with a knife making a diamond pattern.

To make the glaze:

Put the honey, brown sugar and orange juice in a saucepan.

Heat stirring until honey and brown sugar melt.

Brush the gammon joint generously all over with the glaze.

Put the joint back in the oven for 10-15 minutes until the glaze browns.

Serve the ham hot for the first meal.

Later it can be served cold.

Oven: 350°F/180°C Gas Mark 4

CIDER CREAMED PORK WITH CARROTS AND MUSHROOMS

Serves 4

1 lb (450 g) pork fillet
2 oz (50 g) butter or margarine
2 oz (50 g) flour
2 medium onions
8 oz (225 g) carrots
8 oz (225 g) button mushrooms
½ pint (300 ml/ 1¼ cups) dry cider
½ pint (300 ml/ 1¼ cups) meat stock
¼ pint (150 ml/ ⅔ cup) single cream
Salt and black pepper

Cut the pork into four portions.

Melt the butter in a frying pan.

Fry the pork in the hot fat for a few minutes turning to seal on both sides.

Remove the meat and put it in a casserole.

Peel and slice the onions and carrots.

Put the onions in the hot fat in the frying pan and cook gently until tender.

Remove the onions from the pan, and add to the casserole.

Add the flour to the fat in the pan and cook for one minute, stirring.

Mix the cider and meat stock together.

Gradually add the stock to the pan, stirring continuously.

Bring to the boil, add the seasoning to taste, and cook for a few minutes.

Pour the stock into the casserole.

Add the carrots.

Cover the casserole and cook in the oven for 45 minutes.

Add the mushrooms and continue cooking for a further 15 minutes.

Stir in the cream just before serving.

Oven: 350°F/180°C Gas Mark 4

BATH CHAPS

Bath Chaps are pig's cheeks cured and smoked like bacon. Bath Chaps originally came from a breed of West Country pigs called Gloucester Old Spot, which used to feed on windfall apples from the local orchards.

Bath chaps first became popular in Bath during the 18th century because of the city's proximity to the important pig breeding regions of Wiltshire and Gloucestershire. Bath Chaps are sold, cooked and breadcrumbed, in Bath.

1 Bath chap
Small onion
2 cloves
Golden breadcrumbs

Put the chap into a saucepan and cover with water.

Peel the onion and stick the cloves into it.

Put the onion in with the chap.

Bring to the boil.

Skim off any scum.

Simmer gently until cooked, allow 20 minutes per lb of meat, plus 20 minutes extra.

Leave the chap to cool in the water.

Take out of the water and remove the skin.

Roll the chap in the breadcrumbs.

Slice and serve hot with parsley sauce, or cold with pickle.

FAGGOTS

Serves 4

Somerset claims to be the birthplace of faggots. A faggot oven can be seen in the original kitchen in the cellars under Sally Lunn's house in Bath. In the last century, faggots were also known as savoury duck or poor man's goose. Faggots were sold in almost every pork butchers shop.

Traditionally faggots are cooked in a pig's caul (part of the stomach) which is cut into 4 inch squares. The mixture is put into the middle and then the faggots are shaped into balls before baking.

1 lb (450 g) pigs liver
2 onions
4 oz (100 g) bacon
1 teaspoon mixed herbs
Salt and pepper
1 large egg
3 oz (75 g) breadcrumbs
A little milk to mix

Mince the liver, onions and bacon.

Stir in the herbs.

Season the mixture with salt and pepper.

Add the breadcrumbs.

Beat the egg.

Mix the egg into the mixture and stir to give a stiff consistency, adding a little milk if more liquid is required.

Grease a baking tin.

Press the mixture into the tin.

Cover the tin with a foil lid and bake in a hot oven for ¾ hour or until browned.

Cut into squares to serve with gravy and vegetables, or slice and fry and serve with fried eggs for breakfast.

Also good to eat cold.

Oven: 400°F/200°C Gas Mark 6

SOMERSET RAREBIT

Although it must be assumed that the original of this dish is the Welsh Rarebit dating back to the 18th century, other regions have their own speciality, using local cheeses.

Serves 4 as a meal, 8 as a savoury or 'beginning' to a meal.

8 oz (225 g) Cheddar cheese
1 oz (25 g) butter or margarine
1 oz (25 g) plain flour
1 teaspoon dry mustard
2 tablespoons dry cider or beer
½ teaspoon salt
Pepper
4 rounds of buttered toast
2 tomatoes

Grate the cheese.

Melt the fat in a saucepan.

Stir in the flour and mustard.

Add the cider still stirring.

Add the grated cheese.

Season to taste.

Cook gently stirring until the cheese melts.

Spread the cheese mixture onto the freshly made buttered toast.

Slice the tomatoes.

Lay the tomatoes on top of the cheese.

Brown under a hot grill until the cheese is bubbling.

Serve hot.

CHEDDAR CHEESE OMELET

Makes 1

2 eggs
Salt and pepper
1 dessertspoon milk
1 dessertspoon water
2 tablespoons grated Cheddar cheese
1 oz (25 g) butter or margarine

Beat the eggs with salt and pepper to taste.

Beat in the milk and water.

Heat the fat in a small omelet or frying pan, tilting the pan to coat bottom and sides.

Pour in the eggs, shaking the pan.

Allow to set.

Loosen round the edges of the pan with a spatula.

Allow to set.

When the underneath is golden brown but the top is fluffy sprinkle on the grated cheese.

Fold the omelet over.

Serve and eat at once.

Cooking time: a few minutes

CHEDDAR CHEESE DUMPLINGS OR DOUGHBOYS

Makes 8 small dumplings

Dumplings are known as doughboys in Somerset. Cheddar cheese dumplings can be cooked in and served with soup. Excellent with celery soup.

4 oz (100 g) self-raising flour
2 oz (50 g) shredded suet or margarine
2 oz (50 g) Cheddar cheese
2 eggs
Salt and pepper
1 teaspoon chopped parsley

Mix together the flour, suet, cheese and parsley.

Add salt and pepper to taste.

Stir in sufficient egg to the mixture to give a soft dough.

Turn the dough onto a floured board and form into eight small balls.

Drop the dumplings on the top of a stew for the last 20 minutes of cooking time.

If margarine is preferred use the following method to begin:

Add the salt and pepper to the flour.

Beat the margarine until creamy.

Mix it thoroughly into the flour until ingredients are well blended.

Stir in the cheese and parsley.

Beat the eggs together.

Stir in sufficient egg to the mixture to give a soft dough.

Now continue as for suet dumplings.

CREAMY ONION PIE WITH CHEESE PASTRY

For the cheese pastry:
8 oz (225 g) plain flour
4 oz (100 g) margarine or butter
½ teaspoon salt
½ teaspoon mustard
Pinch of pepper
4 oz (100 g) Cheddar cheese
2 eggs
1 tablespoon water

For the filling:
10 fl oz (300 ml/1¼ cups) milk
A bay leaf
2 oz (50 g) butter or margarine
3 medium onions
3 oz (75 g) fresh white breadcrumbs
2 eggs
Salt and pepper
2 fl oz (3 tbls/ ¼ cup) clotted or double cream
2 oz (50 g) grated Cheddar cheese

To make the cheese pastry:

Sieve the flour, salt, mustard and pepper together.

Rub in the margarine or butter until the mixture resembles fine breadcrumbs.

Grate the cheese finely.

Stir the cheese into the mixture.

Beat the egg yolk with the water.

Mix to a dough with the egg mixture.

Knead until smooth.

Roll the pastry out on a floured board.

Grease an 8 inch flan or pie dish.

Line the dish with the pastry.

To make the creamy onion filling:

Put the milk and bay leaf in a saucepan.

Bring to just below boiling point.

Leave liquid to infuse for 10 minutes.

Peel and thinly slice the onions.

Melt the fat in a saucepan.

Add the onions.

Cook gently for a few minutes.

Put the breadcrumbs in a basin.

Remove the bay leaf from the milk and pour on to the breadcrumbs.

Add the onions and fat from the saucepan.

Beat the eggs together.

Stir in the beaten eggs.

Season with salt and pepper to taste.

Stir in the cream.

Put the mixture into the pastry case.

Bake in a moderately hot oven for about 25 minutes or until filling is golden brown and set.

Remove from the oven.

Sprinkle top of pie with grated cheddar cheese.

Brown under grill for 1 or 2 minutes until the cheese topping is bubbling.

Delicious hot or cold.

Oven: 375°F/190°C Gas Mark 5

CHEDDAR CHEESE STRAWS

4 oz (100 g) plain flour
½ teaspoon dry mustard
A pinch of salt
A pinch of cayenne pepper
2 oz (50 g) margarine or butter
3 oz (75 g) Cheddar cheese
1 egg
A little water, if required

Sieve the flour with the dry mustard, salt and pepper.

Rub the fat into the flour until the mixture resembles fine breadcrumbs.

Finely grate the cheese and mix the cheese into the mixture.

Separate the egg.

Beat the egg yolk and stir it into the mixture to give a fairly stiff dough.

If more liquid is required to obtain the right consistency, add a little cold water.

Roll out the pastry into a rectangular shape about ¼ inch thick on a floured board.

Cut the remainder of the pastry into strips of even length (about 4 inch) and thickness (5 cm).

Some of the strips can be twisted to give a decorative effect.

With two pastry cutters, say 3 inch outside with 2½ inch inside, cut out about four rings.

Re-roll any trimmings to make more strips.

Put the strips and rings on to a greased baking sheet.

Brush the pastry with the white of the egg.

Bake in a moderate hot oven for about 10 minutes or until golden brown.

Arrange bunches of the straws in the rings.

Serve hot or cold, as a cocktail or after dinner savoury, or as an accompaniment to soup.

Oven: 400°F/200°C Gas Mark 6

SOMERSET CHEESE BAKE

Serves 4

12 oz (350 g) Cheddar cheese
4 large onions
Salt and pepper
6 oz (175 g) breadcrumbs made from grated wholemeal bread
4 fl oz (6 tablespoons/ ½ cup) milk
1 oz (25 g) butter

Grate the cheese.

Slice the onions finely.

Put a layer of cheese, then a layer of onion, and breadcrumbs in a fireproof dish, seasoning each layer to taste.

Pour on the milk.

Finish with a layer of cheese topped with breadcrumbs, and sprinkle with a little cheese.

Dot with the butter cut into small pieces.

Bake in a moderately hot oven for 35 minutes until the onion is cooked, and the top crisp and brown.

Oven: 350°F/180°C Gas Mark 4

STRAWBERRY CHEESECAKE

Serves 8

For the wholemeal pastry base:
8 oz (225 g) wholemeal flour
½ teaspoon salt
4 oz (100 g) butter or margarine
2 tablespoons water

For the filling:
4 oz (100 g) cottage cheese
8 oz (225 g) curd cheese
3 oz (75 g) caster sugar
1 lemon
½ pint (300 ml/1¼ cups) double cream
3 eggs
½ lb (225 g) strawberries

Sieve the flour and salt together.

Rub in the fat until the mixture resembles fine breadcrumbs.

Add the water and mix to a firm dough.

Knead lightly on a floured board.

Grease an 8 inch flan ring.

Roll out the pastry, and line flan ring.

Sieve the cottage cheese.

Mix the cottage cheese with the curd cheese.

Add the sugar.

Finely grate the rind and squeeze the juice from the lemon.

Beat the lemon rind and juice into the mixture.

Fold in half the cream.

Whisk the egg whites until stiff and forming peaks.

Fold the egg whites into the cheese mixture.

Pour the mixture into the flan case.

Bake in a moderate oven for 45 minutes or until set.

When cool remove the cheesecake from the flan dish.

Whip the remaining cream.

Wash and hull the strawberries.

Decorate with whipped cream and strawberries before serving.

Oven: 350°F/180°C Gas Mark 4

GOOSEBERRY FOOL

Serves 4

Gooseberry Fool has been popular since the 15th century.

1 lb (450 g) gooseberries
2 tablespoons water
4 oz (100 g) sugar
½ pt (300 ml/ 1¼ cups) double cream
½ pt (300 ml/ 1¼ cups) custard
Chopped nuts
Sponge finger biscuits

Top and tail the gooseberries.

Stew the fruit gently in the water with the sugar in a heavy saucepan until soft.

Rub through a sieve, discarding the skin and pips.

Allow to cool.

Blend the custard and the fruit together.

Whip the cream until stiff and fold into the mixture.

Place in individual glasses.

Decorated with chopped nuts.

Serve with sponge finger biscuits.

APPLE DUMPLINGS

Serves 4

8 oz (225 g) shortcrust pastry
4 large cooking apples
A little milk
Caster sugar
Whipped cream

For the apple filling:
2 oz (50 g) butter or margarine
4 oz (100 g) brown sugar
A pinch of cinnamon
4 cloves

Roll out the pastry on a floured board, and cut into four rounds large enough to enclose each apple.

Peel and core the apples.

Cream the butter with the sugar and cinnamon.

Fill the centre of the apples with the mixture.

Place an apple on each pastry round.

Fold the pastry up round each apple.

Wet the edges with cold water, and press them together firmly to seal.

Put the dumplings in a fireproof dish, sealed side down.

From the left over pastry scraps, make two small leaves for each dumpling and a small ball shape.

Push a clove into each pastry ball, and press one on top of each dumpling with two of the leaves.

Brush each dumpling with milk.

Bake in the oven for a total of 30 minutes.

To test the dumplings prick with a thin skewer when the pastry is cooked.

Dust each dumpling with caster sugar.

Serve hot with whipped cream.

Oven: 450°F/230°C Gas Mark 7 for 10 minutes
Reduce to: 400°F/200°C Gas Mark 5 for 20 minutes

Three delicious alternatives for the apple stuffing:

Add a few chopped stoneless raisins or sultanas and almonds to the creamed butter and sugar.

Jam or apple or red currant jelly.

Honey mixed with a few drops of lemon juice or finely grated lemon rind and chopped, blanched almonds.

CASTLE PUDDING FROM TAUNTON

From an old handwritten unpublished recipe in the Somerset Record Office at Taunton. The castle at Taunton dates from the 12th century. It was developed as a major military stronghold and has connections with the Wars of the Roses, the Civil War, the Monmouth rebellion and Judge Jeffries. It now houses the Somerset County Museum.

The weight of eggs in butter and sugar and half the weight in flour. Put the butter into a basin and warm slightly but not oil it, beat it to a cream. Add the sugar first then the well beaten eggs lastly the flour gradually, beat the mixture lightly all the time, butter some small cups partly fill them. Bake in moderate oven 20 minutes. Serve either with wine sauce, or with a little of the center of the pudding taken out and some jam put in.

GEORGE AND PILGRIMS TRIFLE

Another recipe from the George & Pilgrims Hotel, Glastonbury.

Amounts depend on the size of the bowl used.

Sponge cake (1 day old)
Strawberry jam
Whipped cream
Sherry
Custard
Whole strawberries
Angelica
Chopped nuts
Almond essence

Place a layer of sponge cake in the bowl and spread with strawberry jam.

Cover with about 1 inch (2½ cm) of whipped cream.

Sprinkle liberally with sherry.

Add a second layer of sponge and jam.

Pour over thin, hot custard flavoured with almond essence.

Leave in the fridge overnight.

Decorate with whipped cream, strawberries, angelica and nuts.

SOMERSET PUDDING

1 lb (450 g) cooking apples
½ teaspoon powdered cinnamon
2 oz (50 g) brown sugar
A lemon
A little water
8 oz (225 g) Madeira cake
1 pint (600 ml/ 2½ cups) custard
2 eggs
2 oz (50 g) caster sugar

Peel, core and slice the apples.

Put the apples in a saucepan.

Finely grate the lemon rind.

Add the brown sugar, cinnamon and lemon rind.

Add a very little water.

Stew very gently over a low heat until the apples become a soft pulp.

Finely crumble the cake.

In a fireproof dish, put a layer of apple pulp, then a layer of cake crumbs.

Continue until all ingredients are used.

Pour the custard over the mixture.

Separate the eggs.

Whip the whites until stiff.

Fold in the caster sugar.

Pile the meringue on top of the apple mixture.

Brown under the grill before serving.

Serve hot or cold.

BILBERRY (OR WHORTLEBERRY) AND APPLE PIE

Bilberries are small dark edible berries that grow wild on Exmoor. They are a local delicacy. The season is from the end of August and lasts through September.

Bilberries are also known are whortleberries, worts, hurts, whinberries and blaeberries. If bilberries are unobtainable, blackberries can be substituted.

1 lb (450 g) bilberries
3 oz (75 g) soft brown sugar
12 oz (350 g) apples
8 oz (225 g) shortcrust pastry
1 tablespoon water

Wash and drain the bilberries.

Peel, core and slice the apples.

Mix the bilberries, apples and sugar together.

Put the fruit mixture into a greased pie dish.

Add the water.

Roll out the pastry on a floured board.

Moisten the edge of the pie dish with water.

Cover the dish with a pastry lid.

Press round the edge of the pastry lid firmly with a fork to seal and decorate.

Cut a slit in the top to allow the steam to escape.

Bake for 40 minutes until golden brown.

Oven: 400°F/200°C Gas Mark 6 for 10 minutes
Reduce to: 350°C/180°C Gas Mark 4 for 30 minutes

CIDER, RAISIN AND WALNUT PIE

8 oz (225 g) seedless raisins
¼ pint (150 ml/ ⅔ cup) cider
1 oz (25 g) cornflour
1 tablespoon milk
1 lemon
3 oz (75 g) caster sugar
4 oz (100 g) walnuts, shelled
1 lb (450 g) shortcrust pastry
A little water

Soak the raisins in the cider for at least 4 hours or overnight.

Mix the cornflour to a cream with the milk.

Grate the lemon rind and squeeze the juice.

Put the raisins, cider, 2 oz (50 g) of the sugar, lemon rind and juice into a saucepan. Stir in the cornflour. Bring the mixture to the boil, stirring.

Cook gently until the mixture thickens.

Chop the walnuts. Stir the walnuts into the mixture.

Grease an 8 inch pie plate. Line the plate with half the pastry.

Damp the edges with water.

Pile the cold filling on to the pastry.

Roll out the rest of the pastry to make a lid.

Seal the edges and make a slit in the top. Flute the edges with the fingers or decorate with a fork.

Sprinkle the remainder of the sugar on top of the pie.

Bake in a hot oven for 10 minutes then reduce heat and cook for a further 20 minutes or until golden brown.

Serve hot with cream.

Oven: 425°F/220°C Gas Mark 7 for 10 minutes
Reduce to: 375°F/190°C Gas Mark 5 for 20 minutes

WEST COUNTRY JUNKET

Serves 5

Junkets, also known as Curds and Cream, have been popular in Britain since the Middle Ages. In the West Country it is the custom to add clotted cream and brandy to the basic traditional recipe, making the dish especially delicious.

1½ pints (900 ml/ 3¾ cups) milk
½ pint (300 ml/ 1¼ cups) clotted cream
1½ oz (40 g) sugar
2 fl oz (3 tablespoons) brandy
Grated nutmeg
1 dessertspoon rennet (use 1 tablespoon of rennet if the milk used is pasteurised)

Warm the milk and brandy to blood heat. (Without a thermometer, this can be judged by putting a well washed finger into the liquid. It should feel neither hot or cold).

Stir in the sugar.

Remove from heat.

Pour junket into glass serving dish.

Stir in the rennet.

Leave to set at room temperature.

When set, top the junket with clotted cream.

Sprinkle with grated nutmeg before serving.

SOMERSET SYLLABUB

Serves 4

There are two types of syllabub — liquid, best of all made with milk straight from the cow milked into a bowl of sweetened wine just as Charles II liked it or a pail of cider or beer, and solid syllabubs. Syllabubs have been popular in England since the 17th century, and there are recipes for them by all the famous cooks of the past, including Mrs Glasse in 1760 and Mrs Isabella Beeton a hundred years later.

Today syllabubs are made by infusing sherry or wine, with cream. The following recipe makes a delicious liquid syllabub.

4 oz (100 g) caster sugar
¼ teaspoon nutmeg
3 fl oz (4½ tablespoons/ ⅓ cup) port
3 fl oz (4½ tablespoons/ ⅓ cup) sherry
(or 6 fl oz (175 ml/ ⅔ cup) of either one)
1 pt (600 ml/ 2½ cups) double cream
4 fl oz (6 tablespoons/ ½ cup) clotted cream

Mix the sugar with the port and sherry.

Stir in the nutmeg.

Heat slightly to allow the sugar to dissolve.

Whip the double cream.

Fold the cream into the alcohol.

Pour the mixture into glasses (ideally these should be tall).

Put in a cool place to allow the wine and cream to separate (best left for up to 8 hours).

Top each glass with a portion of clotted cream before serving.

When eaten, the wine is spooned up through the frothy cream.

BATH GROUND RICE PUDDING OR CUSTARD TART

Serves 4

8 oz (225 g) shortcrust pastry
½ pt (300 ml/ 1¼ cups) single cream
½ pt (300 ml/ 1¼ cups) milk
2 oz (50 g) ground rice
1 oz (25 g) caster sugar
2 eggs
1 oz (25 g) butter or margarine
1 teaspoon sherry or ½ teaspoon vanilla essence if preferred
Nutmeg

Roll out the pastry to line an 8 inch greased flan tin.

Bake blind.

Mix the cream and the milk together in a saucepan.

Warm the liquid.

Sprinkle in the ground rice, stirring continuously.

Add the sugar, and, still stirring, bring the mixture to simmering point.

Simmer over gentle heat for 5 minutes until thickened.

Remove from heat and allow to cool a little.

Beat the eggs together.

Cut the butter into small pieces.

Stir in the beaten eggs, butter and sherry or essence to the mixture.

Fill the baked pastry case with the mixture.

Bake in a moderate oven for 30 minutes until set and golden brown.

Sprinkle with a little nutmeg, if liked.

Oven: 325°F/160°C Gas Mark 3

RICE BLANCMANGE

Serves 6

A popular Victorian pudding.

¼ lb (100 g) ground rice
3 oz (75 g) loaf sugar
1 oz (25 g) fresh butter
2 pints (1.15 litres/ 5 cups) milk
Lemon peel, almond or vanilla essence, or laurel leaves, to flavour

Mix the rice to a smooth batter with ½ pint (300 ml/ 1¼ cups) milk.

Put the remaining milk in a saucepan with the sugar, and butter.

Add whichever of the above flavourings is preferred to the milk to taste — if laurel leaves are used for flavouring, steep three in the milk, and remove before the rice is added.

Bring the milk to the boil.

Quickly stir in the rice, and let it boil for about 10 minutes, or until it comes easily away from the saucepan, stirring all the time.

Grease a 2 pint (1.15 litres/5 cups) mould with pure salad oil.

Pour in the rice, and leave until perfectly set.

Serve with apple marmalade (see recipe), jam, or a compote of any kind of fruit.

HONEY ICED SOMERSET CIDER CAKE

4 oz (100 g) butter or margarine
4 oz (100 g) caster sugar
2 eggs
8 oz (225 g) self-raising flour
1 teaspoon powdered nutmeg
5 fl oz (150 ml/ ⅔ cup) cider

For the honey icing:
8 oz (225 g) icing sugar
1 tablespoon warm water
1 tablespoon clear honey

Cream the butter and sugar together.

Beat the eggs. Gradually beat the eggs into the mixture.

Sift the flour with the nutmeg.

Fold in the flour. Stir in the cider.

Grease and line a 6 inch cake tin. Put the mixture into the tin.

Bake in a moderately hot oven for about 1 hour.

Allow to cool.

Remove from the tin and ice with honey icing.

To make the honey icing:

Sieve the icing sugar into a bowl that fits into the top of a saucepan filled with hot water.

Stir the warm water and honey into the icing sugar. Beat with a wooden spoon for one minute until the icing is smooth.

Do not allow the icing to become more than lukewarm, or it will be dull.

Use immediately to ice the cider cake.

Oven: 350°F/180°C Gas Mark 4

SOMERSET APPLE CAKE

There are versions of apple cake in other counties. It is particularly popular in Somerset, and also in Devon, Dorset and Cornwall. This cake is traditionally eaten either hot or cold with cream in Somerset.

8 oz (225 g) self-raising flour
½ teaspoon mixed spice
Small lemon
4 oz (100 g) butter or margarine
4 oz (100 g) caster sugar or soft brown sugar if preferred
1 lb (450 g) cooking apples
4 oz (100 g) sultanas
1 egg
A little milk
1 oz (25 g) demerara or granulated sugar

Sieve the flour and spice together.

Grate the lemon rind and stir into the flour.

Rub in fat until the mixture resembles fine breadcrumbs.

Stir in the sugar, apples and sultanas.

Beat the egg.

Mix the egg into the mixture with sufficient milk to give a stiff consistency. (Avoid making the mixture too wet).

Put the mixture into a greased 7 inch round cake tin.

Sprinkle demerara or granulated sugar over top of cake.

Bake in moderate oven for 1-1½ hours until golden brown and firm.

Cool for at least 10 minutes before removing from the tin.

Oven: 350°F/180°C Gas Mark 4

ICED SOMERSET APPLE SAUCE CAKE

1 lb (450 g) cooking apples
4 oz (100 g) margarine or butter
8 oz (225 g) brown sugar
1 egg
4 oz (100 g) seedless raisins
8 oz (225 g) self-raising flour
½ teaspoon powdered cinnamon
½ teaspoon powdered cloves
½ teaspoon powdered nutmeg
½ teaspoon salt

For the butter icing:

3 oz (75 g) butter
6 oz (175 g) icing sugar
2 drops of vanilla essence

Peel, core and slice the apples.

Put in a saucepan with the butter or margarine.

Cook very gently for 10 minutes or until tender.

Rub through a sieve or purée in a blender,

Cream the butter and sugar together.

Beat the egg into the mixture.

Mix in the apple sauce. Stir in the raisins.

Sift the flour, spices and salt together.

Fold the flour into the mixture.

Put the mixture into a greased round 8 inch or 8 inch x 4 oblong cake tin.

Bake for 1 hour in a moderate oven.

When cool, ice the top of the cake with vanilla butter or glacé icing.

To make the butter icing:

Beat the butter until creamy.

Sift the icing sugar and beat it into the butter.

Mix in the vanilla essence throughly.

Oven: 350°F/180°C Gas Mark 4

SOMERSET POTATO CAKE

This speciality is also popular in Devon.

8 oz (225 g) self-raising flour
½ teaspoon mixed spice
3 oz (75 g) butter or margarine
8 oz (225 g) mashed potatoes
4 oz (100 g) brown sugar
12 oz (350 g) currants
2 large eggs

Sieve the flour with the mixed spice.

Rub the fat into the flour until it resembles fine breadcrumbs.

Add the mashed potatoes.

Stir in the sugar and currants.

Beat the eggs and stir the eggs into the mixture.

Grease a shallow baking tin.

Put in the mixture and level the top.

Bake in a hot oven for 30 minutes.

Oven: 375°F/190°C Gas Mark 5

WALNUT AND HONEY SCONES Makes 20

Honey scones have a very long history in Britain. They were made on a 'griddle' before ovens existed.

1 lb (450 g) self-raising flour
A pinch of salt
4 oz (100 g) butter or margarine
4 oz (100 g) caster sugar
3 eggs
4 oz (100 g) clear honey
¼ pint (150 ml/ 2/3 cup) milk (preferably sour)
2 oz (50 g) walnuts

Sift the flour and salt together.

Rub in the fat until it resembles breadcumbs.

Finely chop the walnuts, and stir into the mixture.

Stir in the sugar.

Make a well in the centre of the mixture.

Drop in two of the eggs.

Add the 4 oz of clear honey.

Gradually add the milk.

Work the eggs, honey and milk drawing in the flour from the sides of the bowl, to form a dough.

Put the dough on a floured board and roll out lightly to ½ inch thick.

With a 2 inch cutter, cut out rounds from the dough.

Beat the third egg and brush the top of the scones.

Place the scones on a greased baking sheet.

Bake in a moderate oven for 10 minutes or until golden brown.

Oven: 450°F/220°C Gas Mark 7

STRAWBERRY SHORTCAKE

8 oz (225 g) self-raising flour
A pinch of salt
2 oz (50 g) caster sugar
2 oz (50 g) butter or margarine
1 egg
A little milk
1 teaspoon finely grated lemon rind
½ lb (225 g) strawberries
½ pint (300 ml/ 1¼ cups) double cream

Sift the flour with the salt.

Add the grated lemon rind.

Rub the fat into the flour until it resembles fine breadcrumbs.

Add the sugar.

Beat the egg.

Add the beaten egg and enough milk and mix to a soft dough.

Divide the mixture into two.

Roll the dough out lightly on a floured board.

Put into two greased 7 inch sandwich tins.

Bake in a moderate oven for 25 minutes.

When cooled, turn out on to a wire tray.

Whip the cream until thick.

Slice 4 oz (100 g) of the fruit into half.

Spread one cake with half the cream and strawberries.

Put the other cake gently on top.

Spread the remaining cream on top of the second cake.

Decorate with whole strawberries.

BATH BUNS

Makes 12

These delicious yeast buns rich with candied peel and topped with crisp sugar are still served in the famous Bath Pump Room, which was built by Beau Nash. The city of Bath was very fashionable in Regency times, when the smart society of the day came to be seen, and drink the waters. Beau Nash put the inscription 'Water is Best' in Greek over the entrance to the Pump Room, but Charles Dickens' Sam Weller in Pickwick Papers describes the medicinal Bath water as tasting of 'warm flat irons'.

1 lb (450 g) plain flour
1 oz (25 g) fresh yeast
1 teaspoon caster sugar
½ pint (300 ml/ 1¼ cups) milk
2 eggs
4 oz (100 g) butter or margarine
4 oz (100 g) caster sugar
4 oz (100 g) mixed candied peel
2 oz (50 g) sultanas, currants or raisins
A pinch of salt
2 oz (50g) lump sugar

There are two stages to the making of Bath Buns — a fermenting batter, and a dough.

Stage 1:

Warm the milk until tepid.

Beat the eggs into the milk.

Keep a tablespoon of the liquid aside to brush over the buns before baking.

Cream the yeast with the teaspoon of caster sugar, and add to the milk mixture.

Sieve half the flour into a bowl.

Make a well in the centre and gradually beat in the liquid, with half (2 oz/50 g) the sugar.

Put batter in a warm place. It will have risen and dropped again in one hour, when it will be ready for use.

Stage 2:

Sieve the remaining (8 oz/255 g) of flour into a mixing bowl with the pinch of salt.

Rub in the butter or magarine.

Mix in the remaining (2 oz/50 g) of caster sugar.

Chop the candied peel and add with the chosen dried fruit.

To combine the two stages:

When the batter has risen and dropped back again, mix it into the dough, and then knead the mixture throughly.

Cover the bowl and leave it in a warm place until the mixture doubles in size (about 1 hour).

Turn the dough on to a floured board and knead again.

Divide the dough into 12 equal pieces.

Shape each piece into a round bun.

Put the buns on a greased baking sheet.

Brush the tops of the buns with the saved egg and milk liquid.

Leave the buns to prove in a warm place for 15 minutes.

Crush the lump sugar and sprinkle it on top of the buns.

Bake in a hot oven for 10 minutes.

Note: Some purists say that dried fruit should be omitted, but a few currants may be sprinkled on top with the crushed lump sugar.

Oven: 425°F/220°C Gas Mark 7

SALLY LUNN BUNS

These cakes are named after Mistress Sally Lunn, who went to live in Bath in 1680. Sally used to bake her delicious buns and sell them in the streets, 'crying' her wares. Her baking soon became popular among the smart society of the day. The house Sally Lunn rented in Old Liliput Alley is the oldest in the city today.

The original ovens and huge dough trough can still be seen in the cellars under the pavement. It is still a refreshment house and sells the famous Sally Lunn's buns, which are baked on the premises to a traditional recipe.

1 lb (450 g) plain flour
A pinch of salt
½ oz (15 g) fresh yeast
1 teaspoon caster sugar
2 oz (50 g) butter or margarine
4 fl oz (6 tablespoons/ ½ cup) milk
2 eggs

For the glaze:
1 tablespoon caster sugar
1 tablespoon milk

Sieve the flour and salt into a warmed mixing bowl, and make a well in the centre.

Melt the butter in a saucepan and add the milk.

Cream the yeast with sugar.

When tepid mix the milk mixture with the yeast.

Beat the eggs and stir them into the liquid.

Beat the liquid gradually into the flour.

Mix to a smooth dough.

Cover bowl and leave in a warm place to rise for 45 minutes.

Turn the dough onto a floured board, and knead lightly.

Divide the dough into two equal portions.

Grease two 6 inch cake tins, and leave in a warm place for about 15 minutes to allow the dough to rise again.

Bake in a hot oven for 15-20 minutes.

Brush with sugar glaze as soon as the Sally Lunns are removed from the oven, and return tins to the oven for a moment to dry the glaze.

To make the sugar glaze:

Mix 1 tablespoon sugar with 1 tablespoon milk.

Delicious split open while still hot, buttered and filled with whipped cream.

Oven: 425°F/220°C Gas Mark 7

WALNUT AND HONEY TARTS

Makes 9

½ lb (225 g) shortcrust pastry
3 tablespoons thick honey
3 oz (75 g) demerara sugar
3 oz (75 g) walnuts
1 tablespoon lemon juice.

Roll out the pastry and line 9 patty tins.

Mix the honey and demerara sugar together.

Stir in the walnuts and lemon juice.

Three quarters fill each pastry case with the mixture.

Bake in a moderate oven for 25 minutes or until the pastry is cooked and the filling crisp.

Oven: 375°F/190°C Gas Mark 5

SEDGEMOOR EASTER LITTLE CAKES

Easter cakes is the name given to plain round biscuits with currants. They can be varied by using stoneless raisins, caraway seeds, cinnamon or split ginger in place of currants. They can also be made plain and iced singly or sandwiched together in twos with jam or lemon curd and then iced.

Somerset has several Easter cake recipes. This one comes from Sedgemoor, flat, low-lying land beneath the Mendip hills. It is famous for sheep that provide the famed Sheepskin coats and gloves made in Glastonbury, and for basket making from the willow trees that grow there.

8 oz (225 g) plain flour
A pinch salt
4 oz (100 g) butter or margarine
4 oz (100 g) caster sugar
½ teaspoon cinnamon
½ teaspoon mixed spice
3 oz (75 g) currants
1 egg
2 tablespoons brandy

Sift the flour and the salt together.

Rub in the fat until mixture resembles fine breadcrumbs.

Stir in the sugar, currants, cinnamon and spice.

Beat the egg. Add the brandy to the beaten egg, and beat further.

Stir in the egg mixture, and mix to a stiff consistency.

Put the dough on a floured board. Knead.

Roll out the dough to a thickness of about ½ inch.

Using a 2½ inch cutter, cut into rounds.

Put the biscuits on to a greased baking sheet.

Bake in a medium hot oven for 20 minutes or until golden brown.

Oven: 350°F/180°C Gas Mark 4

CHOCOLATE AND WALNUT FUDGE

1 oz (25 g) butter or margarine
1 lb (450 g) granulated sugar
8 oz (225 g) walnuts, shelled
½ pint (300 ml/ 1¼ cups) water
1 small teaspoon cream of tartar
3 tablespoon plain chocolate, grated.

Cut the butter into small pieces.

Cut the nuts into small pieces.

Put the sugar, cream of tartar, butter and water into a saucepan.

Stir over gentle heat until the sugar is dissolved.

Bring to the boil and continue boiling slowly until the mixture reaches 240°F and is pale in colour — the soft ball stage.

If no cooking thermometer is available, the mixture can be tested by putting a drop in a cup of cold water. If it forms into a soft ball it is ready.

Stir in the chocolate and nuts, and continue stirring over gentle heat until the mixture thickens.

Remove from the heat.

Beat the mixture until it becomes thick and creamy stopping when the consistency changes.

Overbeating makes fudge crumbly and dry.

Grease a shallow tin.

Pour the mixture into the tin.

Leave to cool and set.

Cut into squares with a sharp knife.

PICKLED WALNUTS

The Vale of Pewsey and Bath is famous for walnuts. Somerset's Parson Woodforde notes in his diary of 1788 'I paid her for 400 green walnuts 2.0'

2 lbs (1 kg) green walnuts
½ pint (300 ml/ 1¼ cups) spiced vinegar
1 lb (450 g) salt
8 pints (4.5 litres) water

Walnuts should be green on the outside. To test they should be easily pierced with a needle.

Stir ½ lb (225 g) salt into 4 pints (2.25 litres/ 10 cups) of water to make a brine.

Put the walnuts into the brine and leave for one week.

Drain and cover with a fresh brine made from remaining salt and water.

Leave for another week.

Drain the walnuts.

Rinse and dry well.

Spread out on a tray, and leave exposed to the air for one day till they go black.

Add the walnuts to the spiced vinegar in a saucepan.

Bring to the boil and simmer for 10 minutes.

Cool.

Put the walnuts into jars, filling the jars to within ½ inch of the top.

Cover tightly with a metal lid or greaseproof paper covered with a round of muslin dipped in melted fat.

Leave for 6 weeks before using.

Pickled walnuts keep indefinitely.

GOOSEBERRY JELLY

Adapted from Mrs. Isabella Beeton's 'Book of Household Management', 1861.

6 lbs (2.75 kg) gooseberries (not too ripe)
Preserving sugar — to every pint (600 ml/ 2½ cups) of juice allow 1 lb (450 g) sugar
Water

Top and tail the gooseberries.

Put them in a preserving pan with sufficient water to just cover.

Simmer gently, stirring occasionally, until the gooseberries are quite soft.

Strain the fruit through a sieve.

To every pint of juice (600 ml/ 2½ cups) obtained, allow 1 lb (450 g) sugar.

If a less-sweet jelly is preferred, reduce the sugar to ¾ lb (350 g) of sugar to every pint (600 ml/ 2½ cups) of juice.

Boil the juice and sugar together for about 45 minutes, stirring constantly.

Skim off any skum when necessary.

Test the jelly for setting by putting a little on a cold plate, if it appears firm, it is done.

Allow to cool before pouring into little pots.

Cover each pot with oiled paper, and then with a piece of tissue paper which has been brushed over on both sides with the white of an egg.

Store in a dry place.

APPLE MARMALADE

From an unpublished handwritten recipe book dated 1900-1930 of M. Ross, Baccebro Friars, Somerset.

2 lb (900 g) sugar to 2 lbs (900 g) of stewed apples, weighed before stewing
The peel of 1 lemon very thin

Apples should be put in cold water as peeled.

Boil for 20 minutes or till it jellies.

Put it into jars and moulds and use with rice blancmange.

(It will keep for months).

CIDER SAUCE

½ pint (300 ml/ 1¼ cups) cider
1 oz (25 g) margarine
1 oz (25 g) flour
Salt and pepper

Cream the margarine and flour together in a basin.

Blend with a little of the cider.

Put the rest of the cider in a saucepan with the stock.

Bring to the boil.

Pour the cider into the blended flour, stirring continuously.

Return the mixture to the saucepan.

Cook the sauce over a gentle heat for about 5 minutes until it thickens.

Season to taste.

Serve with white fish or hot boiled ham.

MULLED CIDER AND RED WINE PUNCH

Makes sufficient for 24 wine glasses.

4 cooking apples
3 cloves
2 pints (1.15 litres/ 5 cups) dry cider
2 bottles of red wine
2 cinnamon sticks
4 oz (100 g) granulated sugar
4 eating apples
2 lemons

Put two cloves in each apple.

Put the apples on a baking sheet.

Bake in the oven for 30 minutes.

Put the cider in a saucepan.

Bring to the boil and add the sugar.

Simmer, stirring until the sugar is dissolved.

Add the wine, cinnamon sticks and baked apples.

Heat gently, but do not allow to boil again.

Strain.

Cut the eating apples and lemons into slices.

Add to the punch.

Serve hot.

To Cure Ye Bite of a Mad Dog

In the Somerset Record Office, dated 1735, along with many recipes for good cooking and household accounts, there are remedies for the home treatment of broken belly, rickets, plague, consumption, ague, worms and....

To cure ye Bit of a mad dog.

Take of Rue pluckt f^{m} ye Stalk 6 ounces	of each
of Garlick a little bruised	a Quartr
of Venice or common Treacle	of a Pound

and Shrided Tin...

Boyl all these in 2 Qts of Ale, till it's shrunk a Pint.

To a man or woman give 9 spoonfuls every morning, for 7 mornings

To a Boy or Girl 6

To an Infant 3,

To other Creatures 3 spoonfuls a morning for 7 mornings.